D0853342

[DK] DORLING KINDERSLEY *READERS*

Level 2

Dinosaur Dinners
Firefighter!
Bugs! Bugs! Bugs!
Slinky, Scaly Snakes!
Animal Hospital
The Little Ballerina
Munching, Crunching, Sniffing
and Snooping
The Secret Life of Trees

Winking, Blinking, Wiggling
and Waggling
Astronaut – Living in Space
LEGO: Castle Under Attack!
Twisters!
Holiday! Celebration Days
around the World
The Story of Pocahontas
LEGO: Rocket Rescue

Level 3

Spacebusters
Beastly Tales
Shark Attack!
Titanic
Invaders from Outer Space
Movie Magic
Plants Bite Back!
Time Traveler
Bermuda Triangle
Tiger Tales

Aladdin
Heidi
LEGO: Mission to the Arctic
Zeppelin – The Age of
the Airship
Spies
Terror on the Amazon
NFL: Troy Aikman
NFL: Super Bowl Heroes

Level 4

Days of the Knights
Volcanoes
Secrets of the Mummies
Pirates!
Horse Heroes
Trojan Horse
Micromonsters
Going for Gold!
Extreme Machines
Flying Ace – The Story of
Amelia Earhart
Robin Hood
Black Beauty
LEGO: Race for Survival
Free at Last! The Story of
Martin Luther King, Jr.

Joan of Arc
Spooky Spinechillers
Welcome to The Globe! The
Story of Shakespeare's Theater
NFL: NFL's Greatest Upsets
NFL: Terrell Davis
WCW: Going for Goldberg
WCW: Feel the Sting!
Antarctic Adventure
Space Station
Atlantis
The Story of the X-Men: How it
all Began
Creating the X-Men: How Comic
Books Come to Life

A Note to Parents

Dorling Kindersley Readers is a compelling new program for beginning readers, designed in conjunction with leading literacy experts, including Dr. Linda Gambrell, President of the National Reading Conference and past board member of the International Reading Association.

Beautiful illustrations and superb full-color photographs combine with engaging, easy-to-read stories to offer a fresh approach to each subject in the series. Each *Dorling Kindersley Reader* is guaranteed to capture a child's interest while developing his or her reading skills, general knowledge, and love of reading.

The four levels of *Dorling Kindersley Readers* are aimed at different reading abilities, enabling you to choose the books that are exactly right for your child:

Level 1 – Beginning to read
Level 2 – Beginning to read alone
Level 3 – Reading alone
Level 4 – Proficient readers

The "normal" age at which a child begins to read can be anywhere from three to eight years old, so these levels are intended only as a general guideline.

No matter which level you select, you can be sure that you are helping your child learn to read, then read to learn!

Dorling **DK** Kindersley

LONDON, NEW YORK, SYDNEY, DELHI, PARIS,
MUNICH and JOHANNESBURG

Project Editor Deborah Murrell
Art Editor Rebecca Johns
Senior Art Editor Sarah Ponder
Managing Editor Bridget Gibbs
Senior DTP Designer Bridget Roseberry
US Editor Regina Kahney
Production Shivani Pandey
Picture Researcher Frances Vargo
Illustrator Peter Dennis
Jacket Designer Chris Drew
Indexer Lynn Bresler

Reading Consultant
Linda Gambrell, Ph.D.

First American Edition 2000
2 4 6 8 10 9 7 5 3 1
Published in the United States by DK Publishing, Inc.
95 Madison Avenue, New York, New York 10016

Published in Great Britain by Dorling Kindersley Limited.

Library of Congress Cataloging-in-Publication Data
Donkin, Andrew.
   Atlantis: the lost city / by Andrew Donkin. -- 1st American ed.
   p. cm. -- (Dorling Kindersley readers)
   Summary: Presents the story of Atlantis, the legendary lost
island, and debates whether or not it really existed.
   ISBN 0-7894-6682-1 -- ISBN 0-7894-6681-3 (pbk.)
   1. Atlantis--Juvenile literature. [1. Atlantis.]
   I. Title. II. Series.
GN751.D65 2000
001.94--dc21   00-027359
                                                    CIP
AC
Color reproduction by Colourscan, Singapore
Printed and bound in China by L Rex

The publisher would like to thank the following for their
kind permission to reproduce their photographs:
Key: t=top, a=above, b=below, l=left, r=right, c=center
AKG London: 32 t, Archaeological Museum, Heraklion 33 c; **The Art Archive:**
46 t, Archaeological Museum, Copan, Honduras 16 bl, The British Library 20,
Tate Gallery 21 t; **Bridgeman Art Library:** Christie's Images 34 t; **The British
Library:** 44 t; **British Museum:** 9 t; **Edgar Cayce Foundation Archives:** 39 t;
Jean-Loup Charmet: 18 b, 24; **Corbis:** 31 t, 37 b, Tiziana & Gianni Baldizzone 47 b,
Yann Arthus-Bertrand 29 t, 33 t, Bettmann 6 b, Gianni Dagli Orti 5 t, 14 t, 37 t,
Dennis Di Cicco 19, Hans Georg Roth 28 t, Ralph White 31 b, Roger Wood 36;
Mary Evans Picture Library: 12, 17 t, 18 t, 21 b, 30 b, 35 t; **Werner Forman
Archive:** Anthropology Museum, Veracruz University, Jalapa, 46 b; **Fortean Picture
Library:** 27 t, b, 47 t, William M. Donato 28 b, 40; **Ronald Grant Archive:** 4 b;
Hulton Getty: 32 b, Fox Photos 41 t; **Photo by Shepherd, Minnesota Historical
Society:** 30 t; **Oronoz:** 8 b, 11 t, 16 t, 22; **Pictor:** 25, 29 b, **Planet Earth Pictures:**
Jim Brandenburg 43 b, Chris Huxley 4 t; **Scala:** Pitti Palace 10-11 b; **Science Photo
Library:** James King-Holmes 41 b, **Tony Stone Images:** 35 b, John Beatty 43 t,
George Grigoriou 26; **Topkapi Saray Museum, Istanbul:** 42;

see our complete
catalogue at
www.dk.com

Contents

The legend of Atlantis   4

Athens – 380 BC   6

Truth or fiction?   22

The search for Atlantis 28

The Atlantic Ocean   30

Minoan Crete   32

Atlantis rising   38

Maps of the past   42

City under ice?   44

Atlantis everywhere   46

Glossary   48

DORLING KINDERSLEY *READERS*

PROFICIENT
4
READERS

ATLANTIS

THE LOST CITY?

Written by Andrew Donkin

A Dorling Kindersley Book

The legend of Atlantis

The legend of the lost city of Atlantis is probably the oldest mystery in the world.

It is a story that has fascinated people for more than 2,000 years and has inspired hundreds of books, articles, and films.

Over the centuries, there have been countless expeditions aiming to locate the sunken city.

Expeditions
At least half a dozen expeditions are launched each year by people who want to discover the true location of Atlantis.

Atlantis films
The legend of Atlantis has inspired writers and film makers to use the story as a background for many science fiction and adventure films.

Searching for the fabled lost land, people have dived to the deepest parts of the ocean and hacked their way through the most dangerous jungles on earth.

We know the story of Atlantis from just one writer, Plato, who lived in ancient Greece around 380 BC. Plato included the tale of Atlantis in his writings *Timaeus* and *Critias*, and ever since people have argued about whether this ancient civilization really did exist.

In this book you can enjoy a retelling of Plato's story of Atlantis and its terrible and violent end. You can also read about the worldwide search to locate Atlantis, which continues to this day.

Plato
(427–347 BC)
Although Plato lived a very long time ago, he is still regarded as one of the most important thinkers in history.

Timaeus* and *Critias
Plato wrote *Timaeus* and *Critias* late in his life. Both of these discussion papers feature the story of Atlantis.

Ancient Greece
The political structure of this country was established in about 800 BC. It was divided into a number of independent city-states.

Academy
The Academy was founded by Plato as a meeting place where men could go to study, debate, and discuss ideas.

Athens – 380 BC

The students waited in respectful silence as the old man shuffled down the steps to take his position. Plato, the famous Greek writer and great thinker, was about to give a lecture at his Academy, the first university in the world. The crowd waited for him to speak.

"What do you think is the greatest civilization that has ever existed?" Plato began. "Perhaps you think it is the Egyptian, or maybe our own Greek civilization. Today, I will tell you a tale of a lost civilization much older and, for a while, greater than these.

"The story comes from the depths of history, from a time before our records began. It tells of the rise of a powerful nation, a long and bloody war, and a terrible punishment by the gods. The people's greed led to their city's complete destruction.

Ancient Egypt
The civilization of Egypt is one of the oldest in the world. People lived and worked around the Nile River.

Solon
(638–559 BC)
Solon was a wise and learned man, who wrote a set of new and fairer laws for his country, Greece.

"It is a strange story, which has been passed down in my family. I heard it as a small boy from my great grandfather, who heard it from his grandfather, who in turn heard it from Solon the Lawgiver."

There was a murmur of surprise from the students as the great Solon's name was mentioned.

"The famous Solon," Plato continued, "heard the tale from an old priest during a visit to Egypt. Solon had been invited by some priests into their temple.

"As they sat talking, Solon, one of the wisest of all Greeks, discussed his knowledge of the past. However, one of the priests interrupted him, claiming that Greeks did not know about really ancient history. The priest explained that in the Egyptian temples, there were records cut into stone, which date back further than Solon or any of us could imagine.

"Solon begged the priest to tell him more, and so the priest told him a story that is over 9,000 years old – the story of Atlantis, which I, Plato, will now tell you …

Writing tablet
In ancient Egypt, children practiced writing Minoan and Egyptian words on wooden writing boards like this.

Egyptian priests inviting Solon into their temple.

SPAIN

Gibraltar •

Straits of Gibraltar

MOROCCO

Pillars of Hercules
The Greeks called the mountains on the north and south sides of the Straits of Gibraltar, the Pillars of Hercules. They did not know what lay beyond them.

Poseidon
In Greek mythology, Poseidon, the powerful god of the sea, horses, and earthquakes, used the power of his trident to stir up violent storms when he was angry.

"At the beginning of history, the gods decided to divide up the earth peacefully between them. Poseidon, the god of the sea, received Atlantis as his share of the world.

"Atlantis was a large island, which lay outside the Pillars of Hercules far away in the middle of all the world's oceans. The island's tall cliffs rose sharply from the sea and its lands were rich and fertile.

"Poseidon fathered ten sons, and then divided the island into equal shares between them. They were each given a region to rule as king, but the oldest child, named Atlas, was made king over all the others. Their descendants ruled Atlantis for many happy generations.

"Every sixth year, all the kings would meet at the temple of Poseidon in the island's capital. The kings would talk and give their judgment on important matters. The people of Atlantis agreed that the kings ruled wisely and fairly.

"Atlantean priestess"
This mysterious stone statue found in Spain is called the Lady of Elche. Some people have suggested that the statue with its strange headdress might really show a priestess from Atlantis.

Inside the temple was a fabulous statue of Poseidon in his chariot pulled by four winged horses.

11

1 *Royal palace*
2 *Temple of Poseidon*
3 *Grove of Poseidon*
4 *Gymnasium (sporting area)*
5 *Canals*
6 *Racecourse*
7 *Tunnels joining canals*

Royal city of Atlantis

Plato describes in detail the royal city of Atlantis. The royal family lived in the center of the city. The first ring-shaped island had many small temples and beautiful gardens. The second ring of land contained a horse-racing track and an army barracks for the kings' bodyguards.

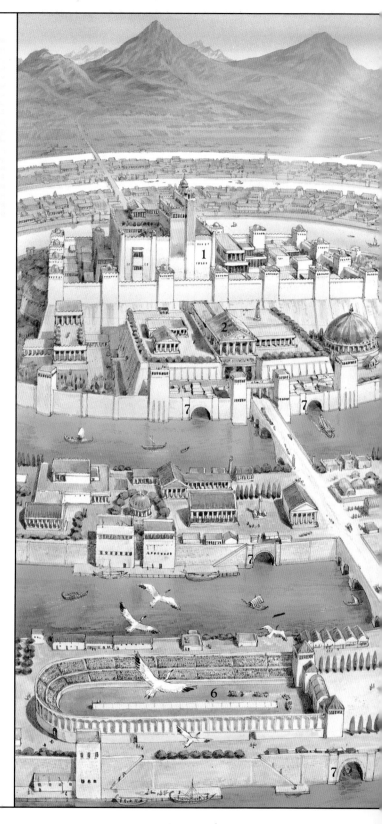

"The most magnificent part of Atlantis was its capital city. At the heart of the city was a central island called the citadel, which was surrounded by alternating canals and ring-shaped islands. Splendid bridges linked the islands.

"On the central island, there was a royal palace, a beautiful grove, and a huge temple in honor of the god Poseidon. The temple was completely covered with glittering gold and silver.

"Sprawling around the rings of land was the rest of the busy and bustling capital where the citizens of Atlantis lived.

Busy harbors
Merchant ships from all over the world crowded into the harbors according to Plato's description.

Orichalc
Plato says that orichalc was a very valuable and rare metal, found only on the island of Atlantis. It was said to gleam like the sun.

"The capital city was located on the southern coast of Atlantis, which was protected from the harsh north winds.

"A long canal linked the city with the open ocean. A ship could sail right into the city when given permission by the kings. Hidden underground canals also linked each of the water rings in the city, so vessels could sail right to the citadel island itself.

"The people of Atlantis were excellent sailors and had long since explored and charted the oceans of the world.

Olives

Grapes

Fish

"Every day, the canals were full of sailing ships bringing important cargoes. The city's many dockyards were never quiet, even at night.

"Beyond the city, there were high mountains and tall forests. The trees were cut down to make ships and houses. The trunks were floated down more canals dug deep into the ground.

Cargo
We can only imagine the wonderful things the skilled sailors of Atlantis brought back.

"The people of Atlantis were rich and happy, but as is the way of mortals, they did not stay content for long. Over the years, the people began to forget how lucky they were, and grew more and more greedy.

"The island had a large army of strong and well-trained warriors. The kings began to send ships to invade other nearby islands.

Jewelry
People have suggested that this unusual necklace found in Spain might have come from Atlantis.

Customs
Ball games and bull hunts and sacrifices were popular in Atlantis according to Plato.

"Before long, the kings were sending their ships further afield. The ships sailed through the Pillars of Hercules and into the Mediterranean Sea.

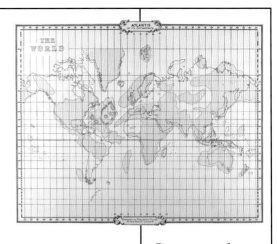

The Atlanteans attempted to invade all the cities in the countries of Europe, including Athens, and to make the people their slaves. Soon there was war!

Conquered lands
Some people believe the Atlanteans invaded and conquered many countries of the world.

"The warriors from Atlantis had expected an easy victory, but it did not come," Plato said.

Earthquake
When the different plates of the earth's surface push against each other, it causes the ground to shake violently.

La fin de l'Atlantide
(The end of Atlantis)
painted by Schroetter.

"Our own forefathers in Athens led a battle against the invaders. Sometimes they joined with others, but when no one would fight at their side, they bravely fought alone. Eventually, the Athenians beat back the invading Atlantean ships and freed all those taken as slaves.

"Zeus, the god of gods, was angry with Atlantis and decided to punish the island's people. He sent a lightning bolt to destroy the city.

"The ground began to shake with the force of a thousand earthquakes. Floodwaters rose and in a single dreadful day and night the island of Atlantis was swallowed up by the sea and vanished.

"The whole island, its palaces and its people, disappeared forever beneath the unforgiving waves.

Comet
A comet is a small icy object that orbits the sun. Sometimes comets, or parts of them, can crash into the earth, causing enormous damage. Could these be the streaks of lightning that destroyed the city of Atlantis?

Exodus from Noah's Ark found in the Duke of Bedford's Book of Hours, 1423

Flood myths
Many cultures around the world have their own myths and stories about terrible floods. One of the most famous stories is the tale of Noah's Ark from the Bible.

"In Greece, we have no records of these terrible events," Plato continued, "because only a few of the brave fighting men of Athens survived. Their descendants were not taught the art of writing, so the memory of the battles with the Atlantean warriors and the heroic victory was forgotten.

"However, in Egypt, records had survived. Solon brought the story back to Greece, and it has been handed down through my family to me. It is a strange but true tale of the destruction of the greatest civilization that ever existed," finished Plato.

Plato slipped quietly out of the Academy, leaving his students lost in their own thoughts. Each of them was thinking of the sunken kingdom of Atlantis lost deep in its silent ocean tomb. Could such a place really have existed?

The fall of Babylon painted by John Martin in 1831

Legends of lost kingdoms
There are many stories of cities destroyed by terrible natural disasters. For example, the fall of the ancient city of Babylon is told in the Babylonian Deluge story.

Stories of sunken cities
Divers often return with stories about discovering sunken cities, but they can never find the ruins again.

21

A codex is a book of manuscripts. The mysterious codex shown here is from an ancient civilization in Central America. Some people claimed that this codex told the story of the violent destruction of an entire civilization, and thought it might be Atlantis. The codex has since been proved to be teachings about astrology.

A copy of a page from the Troano Codex

Truth or fiction?

Was Plato's story true? Did the island of Atlantis ever exist? Many historians think that it didn't.

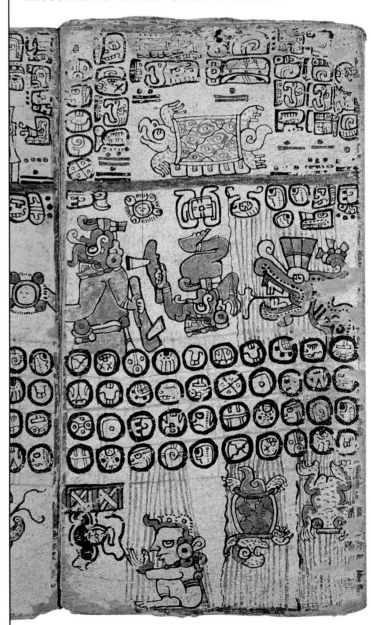

Pieces of pottery from Jericho

For one thing, Plato is the only person to have written about Atlantis. All other accounts are copies of his. If Atlantis had existed, why didn't more people know about it, even if only in Egypt?

In his works, Plato often wrote about human society and his ideas for improving it. Some people think that the Atlantis story is a fable – a fictional story with a moral point. The moral in this case is that the gods punished the Atlanteans for becoming too greedy.

Another reason that some historians refuse to take Atlantis seriously is the date that Plato gives for the island's destruction – 9600 BC. That's 11,500 years ago! Could any advanced civilization have existed that long ago?

First towns
The first town that we know about was Jericho in the near east, now situated in the West Bank between Israel and Jordan. In 8000 BC, it was already a town of 2,000 people! It is therefore possible that an even earlier civilization existed.

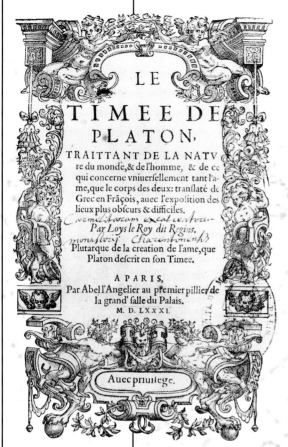

Plato's writings
During his life, Plato wrote over 20 important discussion papers. Many of them contained ideas for improving the way people lived and worked together.

The debate over the existence of Atlantis began within 50 years of Plato's death and continues to this day. Plato's supporters believe that he was telling the truth about a real place that had existed long ago in mankind's past. They point to the fact that none of Plato's many other written works include stories of fake history. In his retellings of the Atlantis story, Plato insists several times that it is a true story.

Solon, whom Plato says originally heard the story in Egypt, was a widely respected figure in Greek history.

It seems unlikely that Plato would lie about someone as important and well-known as Solon. We know that Solon, who was also a shipowner and a businessman, did travel to Egypt just as Plato claims.

But is there anything else in Plato's Atlantis story that can help us decide if it is true or not?

Excavation
In the search for evidence of Atlantis, many excavations around the world have taken place. Sites and buildings have been carefully uncovered.

The ruins of ancient Athens as seen today

Prehistoric Athens
Many centuries before Plato was born, another city existed on the same site as ancient Athens. The buildings of this prehistoric city lay buried beneath the splendid buildings of Plato's city.

Archeologist
A person who studies history by exploring and uncovering ancient places is called an archeologist.

As well as describing the people and capital of Atlantis, Plato's story gives details about prehistoric Athens. Plato writes about a long circular wall, the homes of the best warriors, and a man-made spring that brought water from deep underground.

Historians believed that these details were fiction just like Atlantis, but amazingly, in 1936, an American team of archeologists discovered evidence of them in Athens. How did Plato know?

There are many other pieces of knowledge hidden within the Atlantis story.

Plato writes, "From Atlantis, travelers could reach the other islands, and from them the whole opposite continent." Was he describing the West Indies and America, the continent that lies "opposite" the Mediterranean Sea?

What is strange is that Plato and the Greeks knew nothing about America, so where could that information have come from? Perhaps from Atlantean sailors?

Map showing location of Atlantis
Atlantis has been placed in many different locations on maps through the centuries. This map shows the island somewhere between Africa and America in the Atlantic Ocean.

Astrological world map
The island of Atlantis also features on this strange map, which shows the world divided up into signs of the Zodiac.

Azores
This is a group of small islands in the Atlantic Ocean. Were these islands once the tips of an Atlantean mountain range?

The search for Atlantis
Over the centuries, people have traveled across the entire globe searching for the city of Atlantis. Diving expeditions have searched the bottom of the oceans, while other explorers have climbed mountain ranges and crossed rainforests in their quest to find an answer.

The Bahamas
Could the strange stones found under the water near the island of Bimini be evidence of the ruined city of Atlantis?

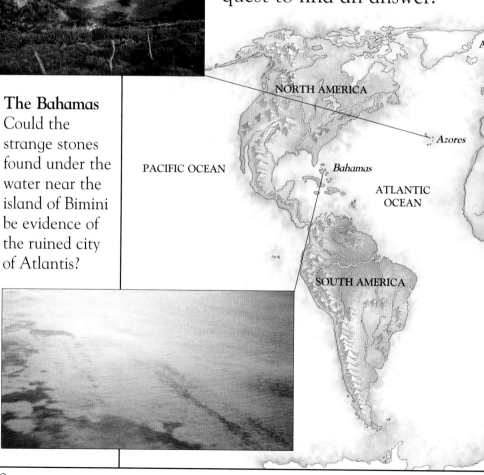

NORTH AMERICA

Azores

PACIFIC OCEAN

Bahamas

ATLANTIC OCEAN

SOUTH AMERICA

Where do you think Atlantis could have been? Fame, fortune, and a place in history await anyone who discovers the true location of the lost island. The map below shows some of the locations that have been suggested. Read about the search to find Atlantis, and see what you think.

Crete
Evidence has been found on Crete that a civilization, which had bull-worshipping customs, was wiped out by a terrible natural disaster. Was this Atlantis?

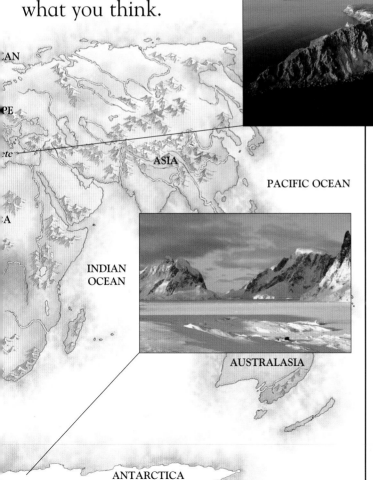

AN

PE

ete

ASIA

PACIFIC OCEAN

A

INDIAN
OCEAN

AUSTRALASIA

Antarctica
The South Pole is the largest area of unexplored land in the world. Could it be that the city of Atlantis was not drowned, but instead lies frozen under ice?

ANTARCTICA

The Atlantic Ocean

The world's interest in Atlantis was reawakened in the nineteenth century by Ignatius Donnelly's book *Atlantis: The Antediluvian World.*

Donnelly, an American politician, became convinced that a group of small islands called the Azores was "undoubtedly the peaks of the mountains of Atlantis." Underwater depth soundings taken for the first time in the 1890s revealed exciting new features of the mid-Atlantic seabed.

A huge range of undersea mountains formed a long ridge running north to south along the middle of the ocean bed. Many of the mountains rose to a height

Ignatius Donnelly (1831–1901) This American writer and politician is remembered mainly for his Atlantis theory.

Ridge graph In 1923, Danish explorers looking for Atlantis took underwater depth soundings from ships to show the shape of the Atlantic Ocean's seabed.

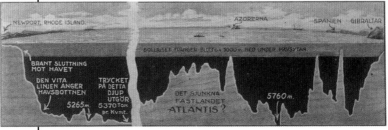

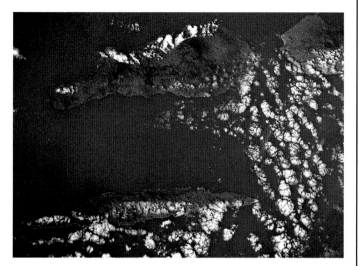

of over 27,000 feet (9,000 meters) above the seabed, and the highest of them rose above the ocean's surface to form the Azore Islands. Were these the remains of sunken Atlantis?

Science has since proved that these mountains are rising rather than sinking and that they were very unlikely to ever have been above the surface. Although Donnelly's thinking was wrong, he had restarted the Atlantis debate and searchers for the lost city began to look elsewhere.

Undersea volcanoes
Underwater volcanic activity can be very dramatic. When water seeps into the volcanoes' vents, it is spurted out again as steaming black smoke.

Arthur Evans
(1851–1941)
This English
archeologist
discovered and
then restored
the palace
of Knossos.

Minoan Crete

In 1900, Sir Arthur Evans, an archeologist, was searching for traces of the earliest civilization in Europe. He was excavating ruins on an island in the Mediterranean Sea called Crete. What Evans found amazed him.

At a site called Knossos, he had discovered the ruins of a huge royal palace built around 1500 BC.

There were frescoes of bulls, and men fighting giant bulls everywhere on the palace walls, as well as some surprisingly modern features like bathrooms. Evans gave the name "Minoan" to the people that had built and lived in the palace.

It was not long before an Irish scholar, K. T. Frost, suggested that what Evans had really found was the city of Atlantis!

Palace of Knossos
The royal palace at Knossos had a total of over 1,300 rooms and a huge central courtyard.

Bull leaping
Bulls were used in rituals and sport on Crete. Plato describes similar activities on Atlantis.

Tidal waves
Huge waves can be caused by volcanic explosions or earthquakes. They can reach up to 90 feet (27 meters) high and travel across the ocean, destroying everything in their path.

Volcanoes
Lava and magma from inside the earth escape onto the surface through vents in volcanoes. Sometimes volcanoes erupt and throw ash into the air.

Frost suggested that the similarities between Minoan Crete and Atlantis were too many to ignore. Both were major sea powers with many ships traveling far and wide. Both had advanced building skills. Both had strange cults, which included the worship and sacrifice of bulls. Just like Atlantis, the Minoan empire suddenly ended and vanished although no one yet knew why.

Decades later, scientists thought they had discovered what happened. About 25 miles north of the island of Crete are the burned-out remains of a volcano called Thera.

Excavations on Thera soon revealed that there had been a devastating explosion around 1500 BC, which had utterly destroyed the town on its slopes. The explosion, scientists claimed, would have sent great tidal waves across the Mediterranean Sea. These tidal waves would have hit Crete and caused untold destruction.

Thera
The explosion of Thera had the force of about 30 atomic bombs. Today, the horseshoe-shaped island called Santorini is all that remains of the collapsed volcano.

Had scientists finally found the natural disaster that Plato recorded in his Atlantis story?

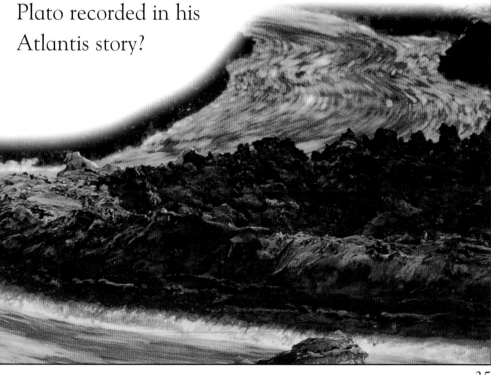

Minoan
Sir Arthur Evans named the civilization he had discovered on Crete after the legendary King Minos. The culture was most powerful between 2200 BC and 1500 BC.

During the 1970s, the idea that the violent and sudden destruction of Minoan civilization was the basis for Plato's Atlantis story was widely accepted by scientists around the world. Finally, they had the answer for the location of the fabled lost land. Or did they?

The "Crete as Atlantis" theory, however, has many problems.

The excavated ruins of the north entrance to the palace of Knossos

Plato was certain that Atlantis lay outside the Mediterranean Sea beyond the known world, and he was also sure that the events happened 9,000 years before his time. Also, Plato and the Greeks already knew all about Minoan Crete and its history and bull worship. It was hardly the mysterious land of the Atlantis story.

Throne room
Evans believed that this was a very important room in the palace, where the priest-king discussed issues with his council.

In recent years, further excavations have revealed that the Minoans did not disappear overnight as first thought. Despite the terrible volcanic explosion of Thera, Minoan civilization continued for hundreds of years afterward.

So, if Crete was not Atlantis after all, where else should we look?

Fresco
Special kinds of watercolor paintings, called frescoes, decorated entire walls of the royal palace. They show the appearance and activities of the Minoans.

Plan of the Bimini Road
The team of archeologists that investigated the J-shaped roadway, or path, just off Bimini island drew a plan of the site like the one shown below. Among the sea grass, a number of stones were uncovered and then examined by scientists.

Atlantis rising

In 1968, pilots Robert Brush and Trigg Adams were flying a light aircraft over the sea around the Bahamas, a group of islands just off the coast of America. As they looked down at the bright blue ocean below, the two friends were amazed to see what looked like a large building submerged in the water. They took a photograph of their find and quickly passed it on to archeologist Dr. Manson Valentine, so he could investigate.

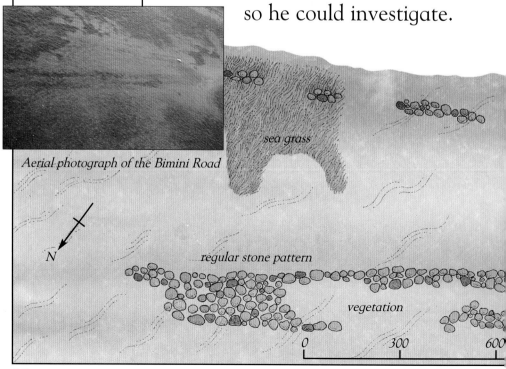

Aerial photograph of the Bimini Road

sea grass

N

regular stone pattern

vegetation

0   300   600

38

Valentine also discovered a long wall or causeway submerged in the water. Were these the remains of the outskirts of Atlantis?

American psychic Edgar Cayce would certainly have said they were. Cayce became famous in the 1930s for giving people psychic readings about their health problems.

He was known as the "Sleeping Prophet" because he would fall into a trance-like state to give his readings. Cayce was fascinated by the idea of Atlantis, and believed he had once lived there in a previous lifetime.

Edgar Cayce (1877–1945) Cayce, an American psychic, believed that escaping survivors from Atlantis moved to places like Egypt, and brought knowledge to the rest of the world.

Previous lives Like Cayce, some people believe that humans can be "born again" after death. So, they may have several different lives.

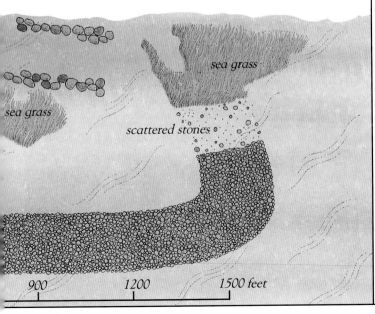

sea grass

sea grass

scattered stones

900   1200   1500 feet

Cayce told his followers about the "Golden Age of Atlantis," which he claimed included Atlantean inventions such as aircraft, electricity, and lasers.

Cayce made many predictions during his life, one of which was that Atlantis would rise again in 1968 or 1969, near the Bimini coast.

Did the discovery of the mysterious wall and the large building mean that Cayce was right about Atlantis?

Sadly, the answer is "no." The two pilots, Brush and Adams, were both members of the Edgar Cayce Association. The only reason that they were flying their plane over Bimini in 1968 was to try and prove Cayce's prediction correct!

The Bimini Road was examined by dozens of scientists, the stones were analyzed, and the area is now thought to be a natural formation and not man-made. The large undersea building has been revealed to be a sponge store built in the 1930s. Therefore, the search for Atlantis continued.

Sponge store
Sponges are made from the skeletons of sea creatures. They are a soft, flexible material that we use for washing and cleaning. Sponges are stored in an underwater building to keep them fresh and wet.

Bimini Islands
The Bimini Islands are popular holiday resorts. Bimini Road is located 2,600 feet (800 meters) beyond Paradise Point on the North Island.

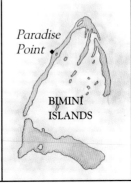

Paradise Point •

BIMINI ISLANDS

Charles Hapgood

This American professor taught at Keene State College, New Hampshire. He began to study ancient maps when he noticed they contained details that should have been unknown to sailors in ancient times.

Admiral Piri Re'is World Map

This map is named after a Turkish naval admiral. It dates back to at least 1513 and possibly much earlier. The map seems to show Antarctica as it would have looked without any ice.

Maps of the past

Early one morning in the spring of 1960, a middle-aged professor sat studying an old map laid out on his desk. The professor was Charles Hapgood and the map presented him with a great puzzle.

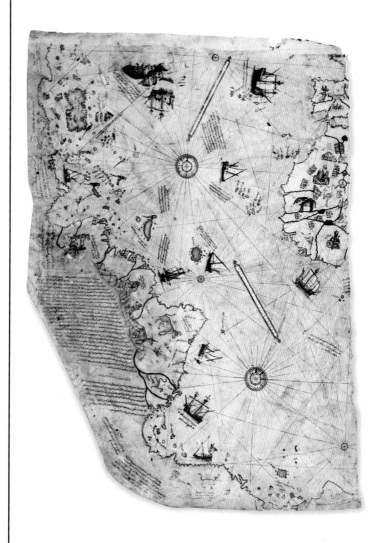

Known as the Admiral Piri Re'is World Map, the document was an ancient sea chart. The map was copied in the year AD 1513 from other far older maps, and yet it seemed to show the coast of Antarctica, a landmass not thought to have been discovered until 1773 by Captain James Cook.

Antarctica
This landmass is situated at the South Pole. It is a frozen wasteland covered by thick ice.

Hapgood showed the map to a friend in the United States Air Force, and was told something even more startling.

The map showed the coastline of Antarctica before it was covered by ice in about 4000 BC. Professor Hapgood was left wondering what unknown civilization could possibly have been advanced enough to sail around the South Pole and map it so accurately?

Arctic
In contrast to the South Pole, there is no land at the North Pole, but it is cold all year round, so the ocean has frozen, forming thick ice.

City under ice?

Oronteus Finaeus Map
Drawn in 1531, this map of the world by Oronteus Finaeus seems to show Antarctica with an ice-free coastline with rivers flowing down from high mountain ranges into the sea.

Two writers from Canada, Rand and Rose Flem-Arth, read Professor Hapgood's work with interest and took his ideas a step further. They suggested that the true location of Plato's Atlantis was actually Antarctica before it was buried underneath ice.

Antarctica does fit many of Plato's descriptions of Atlantis. It is a huge landmass, it lies in the middle of all the world's oceans, and it has high mountain ranges.

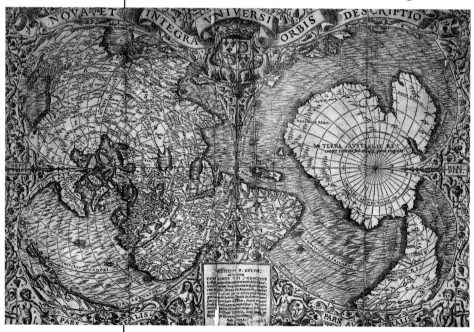

44

The writers suggest that what Plato describes as the earthquakes and floods which destroyed Atlantis were really the results of a massive movement in the earth's crust around 9600 BC. The violent movement spelled doom for the Atlanteans and caused flooding in many parts of the world.

Although the Flem-Arths' ideas may sound unlikely, Antarctica is one of the last great unexplored places on the planet. Who knows what could be underneath the ice?

Earth's interior
The inside of the earth is made up of the thin crust, the mantle, and the inner and outer central core. The crust is between 1–25 miles thick.

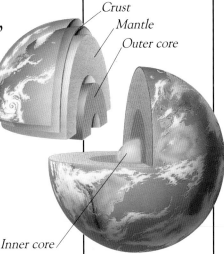

Crust
Mantle
Outer core

Inner core

Atlantis everywhere

Apart from the locations already considered, the lost city of Atlantis is thought to have been found in many other places around the world, from the Amazon rainforest of South America to the coast of Africa. It has even been suggested that the continent of America was Atlantis.

Malta
On this Mediterranean island, these mysterious stones have been suggested as another site for Atlantis. How were such large buildings constructed in prehistoric times?

Olmec stone head, Mexico
Do these giant stone heads show likenesses of people from Africa? If so, it might mean that sailors in ancient times traveled much farther than previously thought.

Other explorers have located Atlantis everywhere from the scorching heat of the Sahara Desert to the frozen wastes of Greenland.

Some people have given their lives to search for the legend. The explorer Colonel Percy Harrison Fawcett led an expedition into the Amazon rainforest to look for Atlantis. He was never seen again.

Perhaps the lost city of Atlantis, with its wonderful canals and huge golden temples, really does lie hidden somewhere just waiting to be discovered. The explorer who finds it will change our idea of history forever. Where would *you* look?

P. H. Fawcett (1867–1925) This English explorer was the leader of several expeditions looking for evidence of unknown ancient civilizations.

Tassilli, Algeria Could this strange mountain range in northern Africa, near Gibraltar, be the huge Atlantean mountains which Plato describes?

Glossary

Ancient
Something that is very old, perhaps having existed thousands of years ago.

Article
A piece of writing in a newspaper or magazine on a particular subject.

Canal
A man-made waterway that enables ships and boats to cross areas of land.

Civilization
A complete human society, which has laws, government, science, and art.

Debate
A discussion on a particular topic between two or more people each trying to change the other's mind.

Descendants
The sons and daughters of a race or related group of people.

Explosion
A violent and noisy occurrence, which happens suddenly and with a destructive force.

Fable
A short story with a moral message to teach people about behavior.

Historian
A person who studies and records history.

Landmass
A large area of ground above sea level, such as a continent.

Lecture
A talk given by a teacher to a group of students on a particular topic.

Legend
A popular story handed down from earlier times, which may not be true.

Location
The position of a city, country, or other feature on the earth.

Politician
Someone elected to serve in the government of a country.

Predict
To say what you believe will happen in the future.

Prehistoric
Anything that occurred before the beginning of recorded history.

Professor
A college or university teacher of high academic rank in a particular subject.

Psychics
People who believe that they can foretell what will happen in the future.

Records
Written accounts giving details about the events of the past.

Sacrifice
The killing of a person or an animal in a special ceremony because of a belief that this will please a god.

Scholar
A person with great knowledge of a particular subject.

Submerge
To dive or place something underwater until completely covered.

Theory
A set of ideas about something that tries to explain what has happened or is likely to happen in the future.

University
A place where people go to study a subject.

Warriors
Fighting people who are skilled and experienced in war and fight for their country, or tribe.

Index

Academy 6
Adams, Trigg 38, 40
Admiral Piri Re'is
    World Map 42, 43
ancient Egypt 8, 20
    writing boards 9
ancient Greece 6
Antarctica 29, 43, 44
archeologist 26
Arctic 43
astrological world map
    27
Athens 6, 17, 18
    prehistoric 26
Atlantean inventions
    40
Atlantic Ocean 28,
    30–31
Atlantis 10, 19, 46
    army/warriors 16, 18
    canals 12, 14, 15
    cargoes 15
    customs 16
    division of 11
    Golden Age of 40
    harbor 14, 15
    kings 11, 16
    legend of 4–5
    priestess 11
    royal city 12
    sailors 14
    ships 14, 15
    slaves 17, 18
    temple 12
    tree trunks 15
*Atlantis: The
    Antediluvian World*
    30
Atlas 11
Azores 28, 30, 31

Babylon 21
Bahamas 28, 38
Bimini 28, 40, 41
Bimini Road 38, 41
Brush, Robert 38, 40
bulls 16, 29, 33

Cayce, Edgar 39, 40
codex 22
comet 19
Cook, Captain James
    43
Crete 29, 32–37
Critias 5

Donnelly, Ignatius 30

earth 45
    crust 45
    plates 18
earthquakes 18, 34
Evans, Sir Arthur 32, 36

fable 23
Fawcett, P. H. 47
films 4
Flem-Arth, Rand and
    Rose 44, 45
flood myths 20
floodwaters 19
frescoes 33, 37
Frost, K. T. 33, 34

gods 10, 19

Hapgood, Charles 42, 43

Jericho 23
jewelry 16

Knossos, palace of 32,
    33, 37

Lady of Elche 11
lightning 19

Malta 46
manuscripts, book of 22
maps 27, 42, 44
Mediterranean Sea 17,
    32, 35
metal, rare 14
Minoan civilization 33,
    34, 36–37

Minos, King 36
moral 23

Noah's Ark 20
North Pole 43

Olmec stone head 46
orichalc 14
Oronteus Finaeus Map
    44

Pillars of Hercules 10,
    17
Plato 5, 23, 24
Poseidon 10
previous lives 39
psychic 39

ridge graph 30

Santorini 35
Sleeping Prophet 39
Solon 8, 20, 24–25
South Pole 29, 43
sponge store 41
sponges 41
Straits of Gibraltar 10
sunken cities 21

Tassilli, Algeria 47
Thera 34, 35
tidal waves 34, 35
Timaeus 5
towns, first 23
Troano Codex 22

undersea
    mountains 30
    volcanoes 31
underwater depth
    soundings 30

Valentine, Dr. Manson
    38, 39
volcanoes 31, 34

Zeus 19